GARFIELD
IN DISGUISE

BY: JIM DAVIS

ℛℛ
RAVETTE BOOKS

This edition first published by Ravette Books Limited 1987.
Reprinted 1988, 1989, 1993.

Printed and bound for Ravette Books Limited,
8 Clifford Street, London W1X 1RB
An Egmont Company
by Proost International Bookproduction, Belgium

ISBN: 0 948456 49 3

GOOD MORNING, VIEWERS. WELCOME TO ANOTHER BROADCAST DAY AT WBOR. THE EASY VIEWING, EASY LISTENING STATION. WE BEGIN OUR BROADCAST WITH THE BINKY THE CLOWN SHOW... HAVE A NICE DAY.

HEY, KIDS!

WHAAA??!!!

WAIT A MINUTE! THAT'S IT! IF I TAKE ODIE TRICK OR TREATING WITH ME TONIGHT, THERE WILL BE TWO SACKS TO FILL, NOT ONE. I'LL GET TWICE THE CANDY!

CANDY, CANDY, CANDY, CANDY, CANDY! GARFIELD, YOU ARE A GENIUS

I KNOW THAT

HEY, ODIE, OLD BUDDY. DO YOU KNOW WHAT HALLOWEEN NIGHT IS?

WELL, TAKE THAT STUPID PUMPKIN OFF YOUR HEAD AND I'LL TELL YA!

THAT'S A NIGHT WHEN DOGS HAVE TO HELP CATS GO OUT AND GET CANDY

AND IF DOG DOES A GOOD JOB, HE GETS A PIECE OF CANDY OF HIS VERRRY OWN!

WELL DO YOU WANNA GO, BOY? HUH? HUH? WANNA GO OUT AND GET CANDY, HUH? HUH? BOY? WANNA GO? HUH? HUH?

OKAY! LET'S GO TO THE ATTIC AND FIND SOME COSTUMES FOR TONIGHT!

JUST BETWEEN YOU AND ME, THERERE TIMES I LOVE THAT DOG

THERE SHOULD BE SOME GREAT HALLOWEEN COSTUMES UP HERE SOMEWHERE, ODIE. JON HAS NEVER THROWN ANYTHING AWAY

I COULD BE AN ASTRONAUT, A ROBOT, A HOBO, A CLOWN...

OR AN ALIEN CREATURE GOING OUT ON THE TOWN

I THINK I HAVE JUST THE COSTUMES FOR US, ODIE

CHOMP, CHOMP, CHOMP

ARRRRR! IT DO BE A LANDLUBBER WHO BE SHOVIN' LASAGNA IN HIS FACE

ODIE, WILL YOU STOP CROWDING ME? THERE'S NOTHING TO BE FRIGHTENED OF

NEVER MIND THAT HALLOWEEN STEMMED FROM AN ANCIENT DRUID FESTIVAL CELEBRATING THE DAY OF SAMAN...

THE LORD OF DEATH

ON ALLHALLOWS EVE THE LORD OF DEATH CALLED TOGETHER THE SOULS OF THE WICKED WHO HAD DIED DURING THE PAST YEAR

HA HA HA

THAT WAS JUST A SEVENTH CENTURY MYTH, ODIE. TIMES HAVE CHANGED. THERE AREN'T ANY WICKED SOULS OUT HERE TONIGHT. THESE ARE KIDS JUST LIKE US WHO ARE OUT TRICK OR TREATING FOR CANDY. JUST LIKE US. LOOK...

SEE, IT'S JUST A KID

OWWW!

SNAP!

SEE?

HA HA HA

I'M NO SCAREDY-CAT

GIMME!!

OH, HOW CUTE! HERE YOU GO, KIDS

ME THINKS YER BE A MIGHT STINGY WITH YER CANDY, MISS. IF YER DON'T RECONSIDER YOUR CONTRIBUTION I'LL GIVE YER LIVING ROOM DRAPES A TASTE OF ME BROADSWORD

THANK YOU. A THOUSAND BLESSIN'S UPON YER HOME, MA'AM

WELL, ODIE, WE'VE HAD A PRETTY SUCCESSFUL EVENING

WHAT SAY WE HIT ANOTHER HOUSE OR TWO AND CALL IT A NIGHT?

HANG ON, ODIE. I JUST HAD A BRILLIANT IDEA. LOOK AT ALL THOSE HOUSES ACROSS THE RIVER OVER THERE

NONE OF THE TRICK OR TREATERS CAN GET TO THEM BECAUSE THE RIVER FERRY DOESN'T RUN AT NIGHT

AND YOU KNOW WHAT THAT MEANS...

YOU DON'T KNOW WHAT THAT MEANS

ARRRRRR! WHAT HAVE WE HERE? WHY IT DO BE A PIRATE SHIP FOR TO TAKE US ACROSS THE RIVER

I COMMANDEER THIS SHIP IN THE NAME OF ORANGE BEARD, THE PIRATE. FREE THE MOORIN'S AND SHOVE OFF MATEY!!

HEY, ODIE!
I KNOW...
LET'S
INVESTIGATE

IT LOOKS AS THOUGH THE PLACE IS DESERTED. LET'S WARM OURSELVES BY THE FIRE

THIS IS MORE LIKE IT!

ARRRGGGHH!

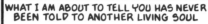
WHAT I AM ABOUT TO TELL YOU HAS NEVER BEEN TOLD TO ANOTHER LIVING SOUL

KABOOM

THIS ISLAND HAS A SECRET... A DEEP, DARK SECRET IT HAS HELD FOR A HUNDRED YEARS. ONE HUNDRED YEARS AGO TONIGHT, A RUTHLESS BAND OF PIRATES HELD UP IN THIS VERY HOUSE. THEY HAD LOOTED MANY SHIPS AND WERE PURSUED BY GOVERNMENT TROOPS

THEY WERE HEAVILY LADEN WITH THEIR ILL-GOTTEN GAINS. THEY HAD TO BURY THE TREASURE BEFORE MAKING THEIR ESCAPE. HOWEVER, BEFORE THEY LEFT THIS ISLAND ON THAT STORMY NIGHT, THEY SIGNED A CONTRACT WRITTEN IN BLOOD...

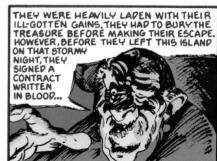

THEY VOWED TO RETURN FOR THE TREASURE 100 YEARS FROM HALLOWEEN NIGHT... AT THE STROKE OF MIDNIGHT... EVEN IF IT MEANT RETURNING FROM THE GRAVE

KA-BOOM!

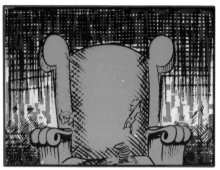

RATS! THERE GOES OUR BOAT

RATS!! THERE GOES MY CANDY

MY BOAT'S GONE, MY CANDY'S GONE. PIRATES ARE COMING ANY MINUTE, IT'S PAST MY BEDTIME

I WANNA GO HOME

IT'S MIDNIGHT... HA! JUST AS I SUSPECTED THAT OLD MAN WAS JUST SOME KIND OF A LUNATIC

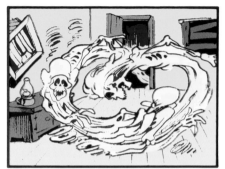

SCREEEEECH!!

CREEEE-E-E-K

CRACK!

THIS IS IT, PAL. WE SWIM FOR IT!

ONE, TWO, THREE

THE OLD MAN WAS RIGHT, ODIE. THIS WAS THE WORST NIGHT OF MY LIFE. I'VE HAD NIGHTMARES THAT LOOKED LIKE BIRTH-DAY PARTIES COMPARED TO TONIGHT

TAP! TAP!

CAROLYN

WELL, LOOKY HERE. IT DO BE ME CANDY! ARRRRRR! I GUESS THIS STORY DO HAVE A HAPPY ENDING, AFTER ALL MATEY. LET'S BE SHOVEN' OFF FER HOME NOW.

ODIE... I'M ABOUT TO DO SOMETHING THAT IS TOTALLY OUT OF CHARACTER FOR ME, BUT SEEING AS HOW YOU SAVED MY LIFE ABOUT EIGHTEEN ZILLION TIMES TONIGHT,

I WANT TO GIVE YOU SOMETHING. SOMETHING OF GREAT PERSONAL WORTH. SOMETHING THAT REPRESENTS A GREAT PERSONAL SACRIFICE ON MY PART...

(SIGH) HERE'S YOUR HALF OF THE CANDY

A selection of Garfield books published by Ravette

Garfield Colour TV Specials

Garfield On The Town	£2.95
Here Comes Garfield	£2.95
Garfield In The Rough	£2.95
Garfield Goes To Hollywood	£2.95
A Garfield Christmas	£2.95
Garfield's Thanksgiving	£2.95
Garfield In Paradise	£2.95
Garfield's Feline Fantasies	£2.95
Garfield Gets A Life	£2.95
The Second Garfield Treasury	£5.95
The Third Garfield Treasury	£5.95
The Fourth Garfield Treasury	£5.95
The Fifth Garfield Treasury	£5.95
Garfield Weekend Away	£4.95
Garfield Book of Cat Names	£2.50
Garfield Best Ever	£4.95
Garfield The Easter Bunny	£3.95
Garfield How To Party	£3.95
Garfield Selection	£5.95
Garfield His 9 Lives	£5.95
The Garfield Diet Book	£4.95
The Garfield Exercise Book	£4.95
The Garfield Book of Love	£2.99
The Garfield Birthday Book	£3.99

Garfield Pocket books

No. 1 Garfield The Great Lover	£2.50
No. 2 Garfield Why Do You Hate Mondays?	£2.50
No. 3 Garfield Does Pooky Need You?	£2.50
No. 4 Garfield Admit It Odie's OK!	£2.50
No. 5 Garfield Two's Company	£2.50
No. 6 Garfield What's Cooking?	£2.50
No. 7 Garfield Who's Talking?	£2.50
No. 8 Garfield Strikes Again	£2.50
No. 9 Garfield Here's Looking At You	£2.50
No. 10 Garfield We Love You Too	£2.50
No. 11 Garfield Here We Go Again	£2.50
No. 12 Garfield Life and Lasagne	£2.50
No. 13 Garfield In The Pink	£2.50
No. 14 Garfield Just Good Friends	£2.50
No. 15 Garfield Plays It Again	£2.50
No. 16 Garfield Flying High	£2.50
No. 17 Garfield On Top Of The World	£2.50
No. 18 Garfield Happy Landings	£2.50
No. 19 Garfield Going Places	£2.50
No. 20 Garfield Le Magnifique	£2.50
No. 21 Garfield In The Fast Lane	£2.50
No. 22 Garfield In Tune	£2.50
No. 23 Garfield The Reluctant Romeo	£2.50
No. 24 Garfield With Love From Me To You	£2.50
No. 25 Garfield A Gift For You	£2.50
No. 26 Garfield Great Impressions	£2.50

All these books are available at your local bookshop or newsagent, or can be ordered direct from the publisher. Just tick the titles you require and fill in the form below. Prices and availability subject to change without notice.

Ravette Books, P.O. Box 11, Falmouth, Cornwall, TR10 9EN.
Please send a cheque or postal order for the value of the book, and add the following for postage and packing:
UK including BFPO — £1.00 per order. OVERSEAS, including EIRE — £2.00 per order.
OR Please debit this amount from my Access/Visa Card (delete as appropriate).

CARD NUMBER

AMOUNT £ . . . . EXPIRY DATE . . . . SIGNED . . . .

NAME . . . . ADDRESS . . . .

. . . .